Kindle Paperwhite Tips, Tricks, and Traps:

A How-To Tutorial for the Kindle Paperwhite

Edward Jones

Revised (print) edition publication date June 16, 2014

Digital rights provided by agreement to

Amazon Digital Services, Inc.

Print rights provided by agreement to

CreateSpace, an Amazon company

No part of this book may be reproduced, stored within a retrieval system, or transmitted without the express permission of the publisher. All rights reserved.

INTRODUCTION

Welcome to Kindle Paperwhite Tips, Tricks and Traps, a combination of a fast up-and-running user guide and valuable collection of techniques to follow as well as pitfalls to avoid.

You will learn all the insider secrets to effectively use your Kindle Paperwhite, ways to improve the operation of your Kindle Paperwhite, and things to avoid that will help prevent problems while using your Kindle Paperwhite. Among the points that this book will show you are:

- How to get around within the user interface and use the toolbars and screen regions more efficiently
- How to make your Kindle Paperwhite your own, customizing its display and operation for fastest and easiest use
- How to find THOUSANDS of FREE (as in, 'zero dollars and zero cents') books
- How to use Amazon's free 'Send to Kindle' service to move Word documents, Adobe PDF files, and images onto your Kindle Paperwhite
- How to setup the security options to protect your account information
- What to do when your Kindle Paperwhite doesn't behave as it should

You will learn all of the above and more, with Kindle Paperwhite Tips, Tricks and Traps: A How-To Tutorial for the Kindle Paperwhite as a part of your library. Read on, and learn 100% of what you need to know to get the most out of your Kindle Paperwhite!

Interspersed throughout many chapters of this book, you will find a number of topics that begin with the headings tips, tricks, or traps.

Tips are techniques that make things easier in terms of use, in a particular area.

Tricks are techniques that change the operation of your Kindle Paperwhite in a particular area, often providing capabilities or performance improvements that just were not there out of the box.

Traps are "gotchas," things to watch out for, that can cause problems.

Table of Contents

Chapter 1: Kindle Paperwhite Out of the Box 7
    Setting up your new tablet: simplicity itself 8
    Getting Familiar with your Kindle Paperwhite 10
    More on Connecting to Wi-Fi 10
    Charging your Kindle Paperwhite 12
    Troubleshooting 13
    History of the Kindle Paperwhite 14
Chapter 2: Using the User Interface: The Window to Your Kindle Paperwhite 17
    It's all in the touch 17
    No Place Like HOME… 18
    Using the Kindle Paperwhite Keyboard 19
    Using the Touch Zones of the Paperwhite Screen 22
    Assorted Tips and Tricks of the Paperwhite User Interface 24
    Using the Toolbar Options 30
    About the Reading toolbar 31
    About the Reading Navigation toolbar 33
    About the Periodicals toolbar 33
    About the Status indicators 34
    Changing your Paperwhite Settings 36
Chapter 3: Let's Go Shopping! 39
    Buying Items 40
    About Amazon Prime 41
    Where's My Data? (Your Kindle Paperwhite Storage, and the Amazon Cloud) 42
    Removing books from your device 43
    Have Paperwhite, Will Travel 44
    The Best Things in Life are (Often!) Free 45
Chapter 4: Free Books for your Kindle Paperwhite 47
    How to Get Free Books from your Public Library 47
    Amazon Prime and the Kindle Owner's Lending Library 49
    Finding dozens of great free books with the "search on zero" trick 50
    Download Free B\ooks from the Web for your Kindle Paperwhite 50

Chapter 5: Open your Kindle Paperwhite to the World by Managing Files 53
    Send Files to Your Kindle Paperwhite via E-Mail 54
    Attaching Word Documents, PDF Files, and Pictures to E-Mails Sent to Your Kindle Paperwhite 56
    Copying Files from a Computer to Your Kindle Paperwhite 57
Chapter 6: Getting online with the web browser 61
    Creating and Using Bookmarks 62
    Changing the Browser Settings 63
    Sending and receiving E-Mail with the browser 64
Chapter 7: Security Tips, Tricks, and Traps 67
Chapter 8: Battery and Power Tips, Tricks, and Traps 71
CONCLUSION (and a favor to ask!) 73
    Join our mailing list… 73

Chapter 1: Kindle Paperwhite Out of the Box

Welcome to Kindle Paperwhite Tips, Tricks and Traps: A How-To Tutorial for the Kindle Paperwhite.

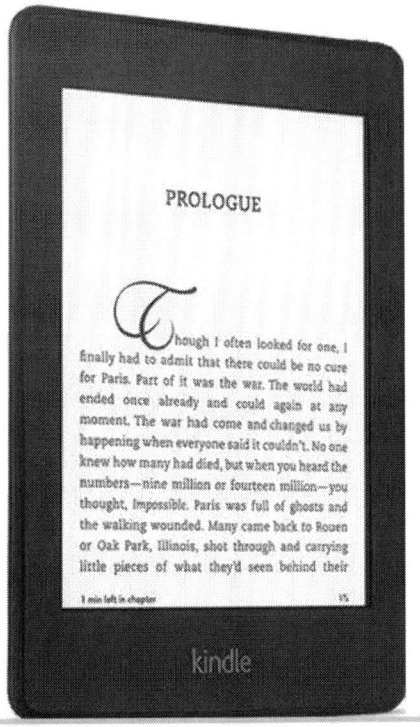

Whether you just received this great new e-reader as a gift, or you bit the bullet on your own in terms of purchase, you have your hands on what has been called (by reviewers at CNN) the "best e-reader on the market." Still, there are things that you can do to make your Kindle Paperwhite work best for you, and teaching you these topics is precisely what this book is about.

When you unpack your new Kindle Paperwhite for the first time, you'll discover that Amazon has made the "unpack and setup" process surprisingly simple—in fact, you may be surprised to see just how few items are actually in the box. Don't feel that Amazon's packing department has somehow omitted some parts; the few items you see are intentionally few, and all that you'll need to get started with your Kindle Paperwhite experience. Inside the box, you'll find just the following three items:

1. Your shiny new Kindle Paperwhite;

2. A USB power cord, used to recharge your Kindle Paperwhite by connecting it to a computer or to a USB power adapter (more on that in a moment); and,

3. A simple single-page "Quick Start" guide.

First things first: look at the following illustration, and locate the power off on switch and the micro-USB connector for the charging cable, both located on the bottom edge of the device.

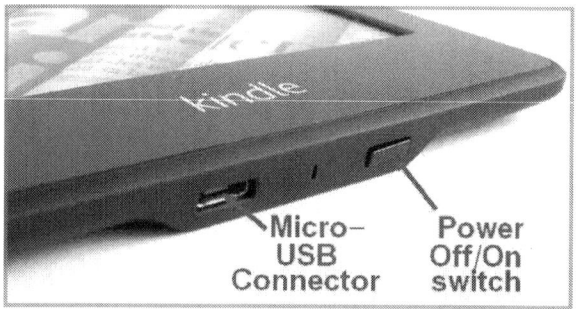

Turn on the power, and determine whether your new tablet has been set up for you by Amazon. If you ordered the tablet directly from Amazon, it has already been set up for you. If you purchased your Kindle Paperwhite from a retailer such as Best Buy or Wal-Mart, you will need to set up your new tablet.

Setting up your new tablet: simplicity itself

If you need to set up your tablet yourself, don't panic. All you'll need is a working Wi-Fi connection, which could be at a coffee shop (trust me on this, I once set up a Kindle while waiting on Amtrak's Acela at Washington's Union

Station). You will also need an Amazon account to register your Kindle Paperwhite against that account.

If you've ever purchased anything from Amazon, you already have an Amazon account. If you ordered your new Kindle Paperwhite from Amazon, you'll discover that Amazon has already set up the device and registered it to the Amazon account that was used to order the device. And if this is the case, your previously purchased Amazon content that's Paperwhite compatible-- books, magazines, and any e-newspapers-- will be accessible for download from Amazon as soon as you turn on the device.

If your Kindle Paperwhite was purchased from a retailer other than Amazon and is fresh out of the box, you'll need to power up your new tablet and you'll need to set it up before you can begin using it. Before you start, make sure you have your Amazon username and password, and you will also need to be within range of an active Wi-Fi connection.

When you first turn your Kindle Paperwhite on, you'll be asked to choose your language. After doing this, you'll select a Wi-Fi network and enter a password (if yours is a secured network).

The next screen that appears will ask you for registration information. You'll now need to register your Kindle Paperwhite. Enter your Amazon account details, or, if you don't have an Amazon account, choose 'Create an Account' and follow the instructions that appear on the screen.

Next, you'll get to choose your time zone, and confirm your account information. Make your selections and tap Continue, and you will be given the option to set up your Facebook and/or Twitter accounts. (You can do this now, or skip this step and save this for later.)

Finally, you will see some on-screen hints and tips that will help you get started with your Kindle Paperwhite. If you already have Kindle content linked to your device, that content will be downloaded automatically. All your Kindle books will appear on the Home page of your Paperwhite, under the Cloud link directly beneath the Home 🏠 icon at the upper left (more on the Amazon Cloud shortly).

Getting Familiar with your Kindle Paperwhite

Once you've unpacked your new Kindle Paperwhite, you should take the time to get familiar with the physical aspects of your Kindle Paperwhite. The component parts of your Paperwhite are delightfully simple, and were shown in an illustration earlier in this chapter. These consist of two items at the base of the device, the micro-USB connector, and the power switch. That's all that you need to worry about locating, as far as controls and connectors are concerned. The micro-USB connector is used when it is time to recharge your device, and if you want to connect your Paperwhite to a computer so that you can easily transfer files, such as Microsoft Word documents, to your Paperwhite. The other component on your Paperwhite is the power switch; press this and then swipe in any direction on the screen to bring your Paperwhite to life. Virtually every other action that you will perform with your Paperwhite is done by means of the touchscreen, and the next chapter will explain this subject in detail.

More on Connecting to Wi-Fi

To get the most out of your Kindle Paperwhite, you'll need to connect to an active Wi-Fi connection. This can be at your home or at your workplace, or in any location (such as a fast food emporium or a coffee shop) that offers a Wi-Fi connection. And if it is a secured connection, you'll certainly need to know the password.

Once you are in range of a Wi-Fi connection, it's also a simple task to connect your Kindle Paperwhite. Get to the Home screen, by tapping at the top of the screen and tapping Home, then tap the Menu ☰ icon at the far right.

At the Settings page that appears, tap Wi-Fi Networks. You'll see a list of wireless networks within range of your Kindle Paperwhite.

Tap the name of the network that you would like to connect to, and your Kindle Paperwhite will ask for a password. Enter the password, click OK, and you are connected. If you are using a Wi-Fi connection at your home or small office, you should only need to perform this step one time. Unless you perform a factory reset of your Kindle Paperwhite or something changes within your Wi-Fi hardware at your home or office, your Kindle Paperwhite will remember your Wi-Fi settings.

tip! Find the password for your home network. If your home Wi-Fi connection was set up by (1)-the cable or phone company tech or (2)-the twelve-year old whiz kid who lives next door, and you have no idea of the correct password, there are a few places you can look to try to find this information. Often, a password will be printed or written on a sticker on the underside of the cable or phone company's wireless modem. If you can't find this information on the modem itself and assuming you have a desktop or laptop computer connected to your Wi-Fi network, you may be able to find the settings already stored in your computer's software. On computers running most versions of Microsoft Windows, you can click on the Network icon at the lower right corner of the Status Bar to open a Network and Sharing Center dialog box, click the Network Properties link to the right of the network name, click Wireless Properties in the next dialog box, then click the Security tab and turn on Show Characters to reveal the Wi-Fi password. If you are trying to connect to a Wi-Fi network in a large office, you'll likely need to speak to your network administrator to obtain this information.

Charging your Kindle Paperwhite

If you thought something was missing when you originally opened the box and noticed a cord with the absence of a wall plug of any sort, you're not alone in jumping to that conclusion. Amazon does not ship the Kindle Paperwhite with any wall plug charger, but the USB cable that did come with your Kindle Paperwhite can be used to recharge the device. There are actually three different ways that you can recharge your Kindle Paperwhite. Listed in order of expense (from no cost to around $20.00 U.S. at the time of this writing), they are:

1. Use any computer with a USB connector to recharge your Kindle. Insert the small end of the cable into the Kindle Paperwhite's Micro USB connector located on the underside of the device, and insert the larger end of the same cable into any USB connector on your computer. The Paperwhite should be turned off, the computer must be turned on, and you can't allow the computer to hibernate or go to sleep. Using this method, a Kindle Paperwhite that's low on battery power will reach a full charge in about 12 hours.

2. Purchase an Amazon 5W USB Charger (click this link for details). Insert the large end of your USB cable into the adapter, insert the small end into your Kindle Paperwhite's micro USB connector, and plug in the adapter. With this adapter, a Kindle Paperwhite that is low on battery power will reach a full charge in roughly 6 hours or less if your Kindle is asleep.

3. Purchase a Kindle PowerFast Accelerated Charger (click this link for details). Insert the large end of the USB cable into the PowerFast Accelerated Charger, and insert the small end into the micro USB connector on the underside of your Kindle. Plug in the adapter, and your Kindle Paperwhite will reach a full charge in 4 hours or less.

Since items two and three both cost approximately $20.00 from Amazon, your choice of either is a matter of convenience. The Kindle power adapter is smaller, lighter, and therefore easier to pack when traveling. Also, note that you can use any compatible USB charger that has an output of 5 volts and 5 watts or greater (or 0.8 amps for greater). A large number of devices, including other tablets such as Barnes & Noble's NOOK, Google's Nexus, and many modern digital cameras use the same type of power adapter, so check the other gadgets that may be lying around your house before shelling out $20.00.

Troubleshooting

Having problems??? When in doubt, reboot. Your Kindle Paperwhite is a sophisticated computer, and like all computers, it may hiccup for unexplainable reasons at times. If your Kindle Paperwhite freezes or locks up and refuses to respond to any actions, perform a hard reset. (You needn't worry about losing any memory settings with this type of reset; it just halts any software currently running and shuts down your device.) Hold the power button depressed for at least 20 seconds and then release the button. Wait another 10 seconds, then turn on your Kindle Paperwhite.

If you are experiencing an unusually high number of system lock-ups, make sure your battery charge level is not very low. A nearly fully-drained battery is a common cause of random Kindle Paperwhite freezes.

History of the Kindle Paperwhite

This final section of this first chapter certainly isn't required reading if you are to become an accomplished user of your Kindle Paperwhite, but it is a fascinating success story. The Kindle Paperwhite is one of a line of products- Amazon Kindles- that all sprang from the original Amazon Kindle, a revolutionary device inspired by a revolutionary individual, Amazon founder and CEO Jeff Bezos. During the nascent days of the World Wide Web, it was Bezos who came up with the idea of selling books online, rather than in the traditional bricks and mortar bookstore environment, and Bezos founded Amazon, billed as the world's largest bookstore. Books were very good to Bezos and to Amazon, catapulting the company to a multibillion dollar global enterprise and taking Bezos to billionaire status in the process. But even though Bezos himself was (and is, according to reports) an avid book reader, he recognized something: a cornerstone of Amazon's long-term future in the 21st century, the printed book, was a likely candidate for obsolescence by the end of the 21st century, if not sooner. Music had gone digital, video was in the process of moving in that direction, and for the printed book, the same transition was simply a matter of time. Having built a better bookstore, Bezos believed he could improve upon one of humanity's greatest inventions- the printed book- by taking it digital.

In 2004, Bezos turned a group of engineers loose in an Amazon subsidiary, Lab126, based in Cupertino, California, and charged them with the task of developing a digital replacement for the printed book. Roughly three years later, in November of 2007, Amazon placed the fruits of Bezos dream and the engineers' labors- the original Amazon Kindle- on sale. It used a patented E-ink display that was capable of rendering 16 shades to simulate reading on paper while using minimal amounts of power. Content for the Amazon Kindle could be purchased online and downloaded wirelessly. (The name "Kindle" was the brainchild of consultants hired by the Lab126 division of Amazon, who felt that like kindling, it had the potential to light a fire- and that is exactly what the device began to do in the book publishing world.)

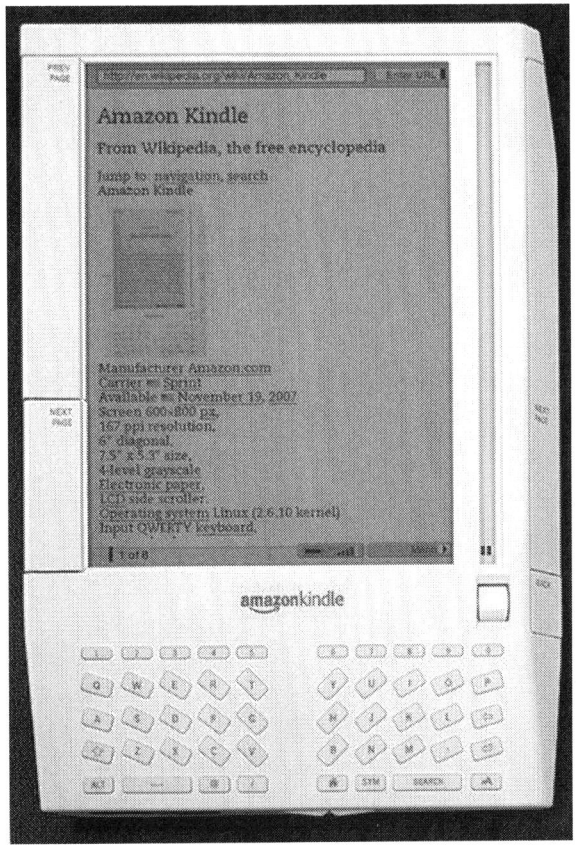

First Amazon Kindle (photo credit: Wikipedia)

Despite the fact that the device cost nearly $400, Amazon sold out its initial manufacturing run in a little over five and one half hours, and the Kindle remained out of stock until late April of 2008. The success of the original Amazon Kindle led to a family of devices, and as technology continued to advance and manufacturing costs continued to drop, the Kindle Paperwhite became another product in the Amazon Kindle lineup. The first generation Kindle Paperwhite was released in October 2012. The device sported a six inch diagonal screen using Amazon's patented e-ink technology, and the Paperwhite (like the Kindle Touch models that preceded it) used a touch screen keyboard rather than the physical button keyboards of the earliest models of Kindles. But the Paperwhite also came with another revolutionary feature that previous Kindles based upon the e-ink technology lacked-- a backlight. The built-in backlight enables Paperwhite readers to read books even in low light or no-light situations.

In September of 2013, Amazon released the next generation Kindle Paperwhite, with a higher contrast e-ink screen, improved back lighting, an integrated dictionary and Wikipedia lookup, and a feature that lets you flip forwards or backwards by pages in a popup window and then return to your original reading location. That model of Paperwhite is the Paperwhite that's described in this book.

Concurrently, Amazon has released Kindle Fires, which unlike the Kindle Paperwhite, are LCD based color screen tablet devices. Hence they do not have the battery life of a Kindle Paperwhite, but they do allow for viewing of movies and TV shows and other digital content in addition to the reading of e-books, magazines, and newspapers. Combined with the Paperwhite and the Kindle Fire product line, the Amazon Kindles have become a major part of the tablet market in terms of sales worldwide. And while there's still a number of years left to this 21st century, the handwriting is clearly on the wall with regards to the eventual demise of the paper-based book. The Association of American Publishers reported that in the first quarter of 2012, e-book sales surpassed those of their paper-based counterparts for the first time- adult eBook sales were reported at $282.3 million, while adult hardcover sales during that same period reached only $229.6 million.

Chapter 2: Using the User Interface: The Window to Your Kindle Paperwhite

The user interface (techno-speak for "the way you get along with the device") is simple, efficient, and directly to-the-point on a Kindle Paperwhite. Nevertheless, there are things that you can do to make the way that you use your Kindle Paperwhite more efficient, and that is what this chapter is all about.

It's all in the touch

The touchscreen interface is the primary means of interacting with your Kindle Paperwhite, and it lets you perform a variety of actions with no more than a tap or a swipe of a finger. As an example, you can select an item simply by tapping the item. You can tap a title or book cover on your Home screen to open the book, or tap a button to perform that button's action. When it is necessary for you to type text, such as in response to a prompt for a search phrase, a soft keyboard will appear on the lower portion of your Kindle Paperwhite's display, and you can tap the letters of the keyboard to create a response.

In addition to simply tapping on icons or letters of the soft keyboard, there are specific time saving hand and finger actions that you'll use often on your Kindle Paperwhite, or on most touchscreen devices. These include the following:

Tapping on the Kindle Paperwhite's screen is the equivalent of pressing a keyboard key when you tap the Kindle's soft keyboard, and it serves as the equivalent of clicking a mouse button when you tap anywhere other than on the Kindle Paperwhite keyboard. Tapping on an item or a web link will open that item, or take you to a corresponding website in the Paperwhite's web browser. At some locations (such as when a photo is visible on the screen), you can double-tap to enlarge the image, and double-tap again to return to your original view.

Swiping refers to touching one side of the screen, and while holding your finger on the screen, rapidly moving that finger to the other side. The most common use of swiping is to turn the pages of an e-book; swiping from right to left moves you to the next page of a book, while swiping from left to right moves you to the prior page of a book.

Flicking refers to swiping in a vertical direction, rapidly running one's finger up or down the screen. You will use this movement with long documents, or with book pages that take on a more vertical format.

The two-finger spread: a gesture by this name may have insulting meanings in many cultures, but when it comes to a touchscreen, this refers to a productive finger movement. You press two fingers onto the screen and while holding them on the screen, spread the fingers apart. With most books or periodicals that contain images, this action enlarges what you see on the screen.

The Pinch: Finally, this action is the exact opposite of the two-finger spread; place two fingers on the screen some distance apart, and while holding them on the screen, bring the fingers together. With most books or periodicals that contain images, this reduces the size of the image that you see on the screen.

No Place Like HOME...

From the Home screen, your books and periodicals are all accessible with a finger tap. And there is a Search icon (in the shape of a magnifying glass) that can be used to search the entire device content, or to search Amazon's massive library of content.

Know how to find your way home. One of the first things any young child learns is how to come home, and any new Kindle Paperwhite user should know how to get to the Home screen as well. From anywhere you are at, tap at the top of the screen, and the Home icon will appear at the upper left. Tap Home and you will return to the Home screen.

Using the Kindle Paperwhite Keyboard

By now you've probably become somewhat familiar with your Kindle's touch-screen keyboard. If this is your first experience with a touch-screen keyboard, you'll need to know of some differences between the keyboard on your Kindle and that of a traditional computer. The keyboard is designed to be visually intuitive, so that most users can get the hang of things fairly quickly. At the same time, some adjustments had to be made by Amazon's design engineers to pack all of the needed keys into such a small space, so you'll want to know about the unique features of your keyboard. (The illustration that follows shows an example of the soft keyboard found on the Kindle Paperwhite.)

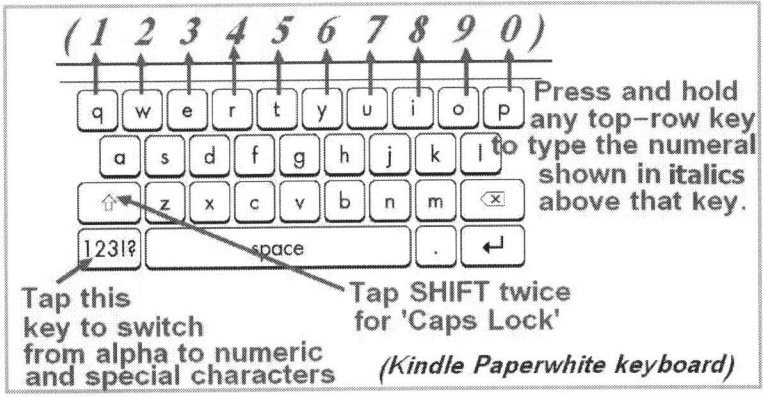

The Kindle Paperwhite really does have a "Caps Lock" key. For those times when you need to type a string of characters as ALL UPPERCASE LETTERS, just double-tap the Shift key, and a small horizontal bar will appear underneath the Shift symbol on the key indicator indicating that you are in Caps Lock mode. Type your upper case letters, then press the Shift key once more to drop out of Caps Lock mode.

Tip! You can change the orientation of the Kindle to make the keyboard larger. Most Kindle Paperwhite books or periodicals can be viewed in portrait or landscape mode, and the keyboard is larger and easier to use in landscape mode. Rotate the Kindle Paperwhite 90 degrees to get a landscape view of the keyboard, for an easier typing experience.

Tip! When typing large amounts of text, end each sentence with a fast double-space. Heavy duty word processing on a Kindle Paperwhite (or any similarly sized tablet) is going to be somewhat challenging due to the combination of a soft keyboard and small screen size. One time saving tip when doing a lot of typing on the Kindle Paperwhite is at the end of each sentence, tap the spacebar quickly twice. A fast double-space will automatically insert a period, followed by a single space. You can then continue on to the next sentence. You'll also want to know about the following tips related to the use of your keyboard:

Tip! Use the numbers shortcut to quickly enter numbers. If you are typing text, you don't need to switch between the letters keyboard and the numbers and symbols keyboard just to enter a number. The top row of letters can be long-pressed to enter a number. From left to right, a long-press on any of the top row of keys produce numbers from 1 through 9, followed by 0. Press and hold a top row letter until a number appears, then release, to type that number.

💡 Use the period shortcut for some commonly used punctuation characters. Hold down the period key until a bar of shortcut characters appear, then slide to the desired character and release your finger to enter that character.

💡 Your finger can serve as an insertion pointer. When editing large amounts of text, tap your finger on any empty area to display the Editing Tool. You can then press on it and move your fingertip within the text that you already typed, then release and edit the text as desired. When done editing, tap again at the end of the text, and continue typing.

💡 Access the Cut-Copy-and-Paste options with a long-press on any word. If you need to cut or copy and paste during text editing, long-press on any single word, and cut / copy / paste editing options will appear, along with two selection handles. Drag the selection handles to highlight the desired text, then long-press on the desired text, and choose Cut or Copy. To paste the cut or copied text elsewhere, just long press at the desired location, and tap Paste.

💡 Let your Kindle's 'auto-entry' feature complete words for you. As you type, you may notice word suggestions based on your entries appear above the keyboard, and you can tap the desired word to complete the entry. You can also switch to numbers by tapping the '123' key, and you can switch back to letters by tapping the 'ABC' key on the keyboard. To reveal an alternate keyboard laded with special symbols, tap the '#~=' key (located just above and to the left of the spacebar).

Your Kindle Paperwhite is fluent in multiple languages. You can choose a keyboard for a different language, if desired. At the Home page tap the Menu icon at the upper right, and then choose Settings from the menu that appears. On the Settings page select Device Options, then Language and Dictionaries, then select the Keyboards option. If you have selected multiple keyboards, a Globe key is added to your keyboard. To choose another keyboard, tap the Globe key.

You can also enter various special characters and characters from foreign language character sets by performing a 'long-press' (pressing and holding) on a given letter until a row of characters appears, then you can tap the desired character to insert it into your text. As an example, if you press and hold down the letter "e," a row containing the following characters appears:

è é ê ë e

and you can tap the desired character to insert that character into your text.

Using the Touch Zones of the Paperwhite Screen

Your Kindle Paperwhite screen is divided into certain areas known as touch zones. These touch zones make it easy to turn pages of a book or magazine while using just one hand. The following illustrations show the touch zones of the Kindle Paperwhite screen while you are in portrait or landscape mode.

(Touch zones while in portrait mode)

(Touch zones while in landscape mode)

Tap anywhere in the largest area, known as the display area, to move to the next page; tapping anywhere within the smaller area on the left side of the screen moves you to the previous page. You can also swipe your finger from left to right or from right to left to easily change pages. Swiping your finger from left to right across the screen moves you to the previous page, while swiping your finger from right to left across the screen moves you to the next page.

As you are reading, you can change the orientation of the screen by tapping the Menu ☰ icon, and choosing landscape or portrait mode. (The option that you see will depend on the current orientation of your Kindle; if you are already in Portrait mode, the menu option reads 'Landscape mode', and if you are already in Landscape mode, the menu option reads 'Portrait mode.'.)

Assorted Tips and Tricks of the Paperwhite User Interface

Give your Kindle Paperwhite some personality by changing its name. By default, your Kindle Paperwhite always displays a name in the upper left hand corner such as Edward's Kindle or Edward's 3rd Kindle. You can change this to something that better fits your personality. To do so, at the Home screen, tap the Menu icon in the upper right corner, then tap Settings > Device Options > Personalize Your Kindle > Device Name. You'll see a screen similar to the following appear:

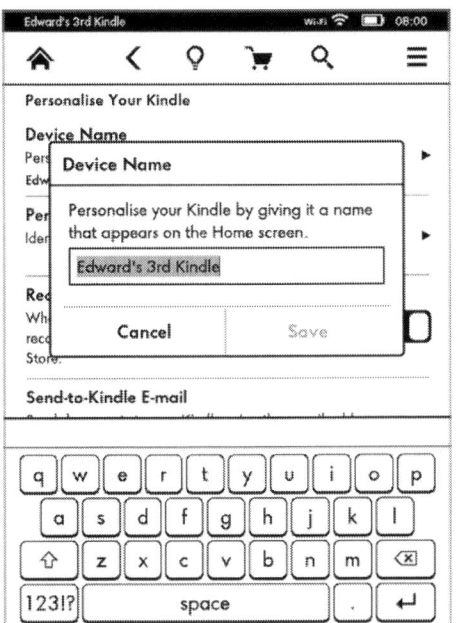

In the Device Name dialog box, enter a desired name for your device and tap Save.

Enjoy Games on the Kindle Paperwhite. While it's true that an LCD based tablet like Amazon's Kindle Fire HD is a far superior game platform, it is also true that you can play games on the Kindle Paperwhite that are designed to run on the Paperwhite. Tap the top of your screen to bring up the menu bar, and tap the shopping cart to go to the Amazon store. In the search box, search for "active content." The result, similar to the example shown in the following illustration, will be titles at the Amazon store that are active applications for the Kindle Paperwhite.

Over 90% of the entries that you will find in the 'active content' category are games, and a number of these are free. (Video Poker, by Amazon Digital Services, is this author's favorite time waster when waiting for an airline flight.) Tap a selection, tap Buy, and the game will be downloaded via Amazon's Whispernet to your device.

Change the reading settings on your device to suit YOUR visual needs. If you find yourself squinting or straining your eyes to read text on your Paperwhite, it doesn't necessarily mean that you need an eye exam. You can change both the font and the font size used by the Paperwhite to display text. Open any book, tap the top of the screen to display the toolbars, and tap the text button at the far left (Aa). The Fonts dialog box, shown in the following illustration, will appear, and you can choose from one of six available fonts, change the font size, and adjust the line spacing and margins used by your Kindle Paperwhite.

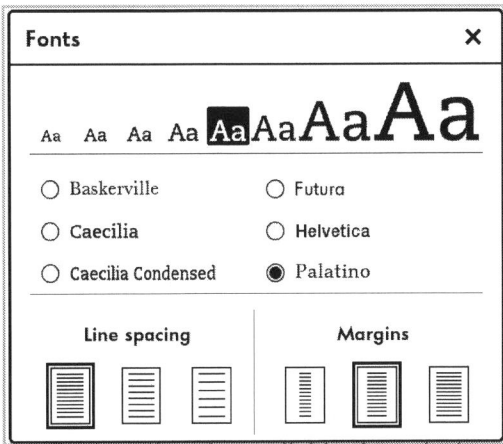

As you tap to choose various selections in the dialog box, the underlying text will change to reflect the overall effects of your choices. When done, tap the X in the upper right corner of the dialog box to close it.

Adjust your screen lighting for best viewing under available light conditions. The Paperwhite's built-in backlighting is a wonderful feature when compared to earlier e-ink Kindles that totally lacked such a feature. By default, the backlighting is set to an "average" position, which may not be the best setting for very bright or very dark conditions. While reading any publication, tap the top of the screen, then tap the Screen Light icon (it's the one in the shape of a light bulb).The Screen Light control, shown here, will appear.

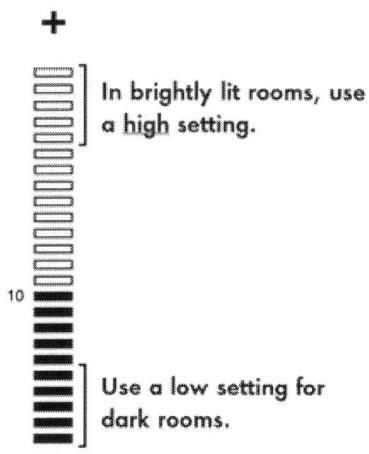

You can slide your finger along the scale to adjust the brightness, or you can press and hold the (+) symbol at the top of the control to set the backlighting to maximum brightness.

Note that even at the minimum brightness setting, some power is applied to the backlighting. The screen backlighting is turned completely off only when your Kindle Paperwhite goes to sleep, or when you power down the device.

Organize your book collection into collections. The Kindle Paperwhite can hold an estimated 1,100 e-books. That's a lot of content, and if you are an avid reader (or just like to take advantage of the sources of free books described elsewhere in this publication), you'll quickly find your screen real estate overwhelmed with more titles than you can easily track. The answer to this dilemma is for you to organize your titles into collections. You can create as many collections as you wish, and you can store books, documents, active content, or any combination of the three within a collection. As an example, you might have a Science Fiction collection, a Romance collection, a News collection holding your electronic newspapers and newsmagazines, a Technical Writings collection, a For My Eyes Only collection (someplace to store that steamy erotica, if you're into that sort of thing) and a "Microsoft Word documents from the office" collection. (In the following illustration, the top of the author's Kindle Paperwhite displays collections created to store different categories of publications.)

Once you create your first collection, your kindle Paperwhite will sort your home screen content by collections. You can use the following steps to create a new collection:

1. At the Home screen, tap the Menu ☰ icon, and then tap Create New Collection.

2. Using the keyboard that appears, enter a name for your collection, and then tap OK. When you tap OK, a list of the items on your Paperwhite that can be added to a collection will appear. (Note: periodicals cannot be put into collections.)

3. Tap the check box beside the title of any item to add it to the new collection, then tap done when you are finished.

You can add or remove items from a collection at any time by tapping the same Menu ☰ icon when inside a collection and choosing Add or Remove from the menu that appears. The same menu also gives you choices for renaming a collection and deleting collections. (If you choose to delete a collection, the items the collection contains are not deleted from your Kindle Paperwhite. The items are simply placed on the home screen after you delete the collection.)

Using the Toolbar Options

Whether you are in portrait or landscape mode, you can also tap at the top of the screen to display a toolbar. The toolbar options that you see vary, depending on whether you are viewing a book, a periodical, or a web page at the time. The options that you may see are detailed in the following paragraphs:

Home: From anywhere, tapping the Home 🏠 icon always gets you back to your Home screen. Your Home screen contains a list of your books, magazines, and other digital content stored on your Kindle Paperwhite.

Back: Tap to move in reverse among the last actions you've performed. For example, in the midst of a magazine article, you might tap a link to jump to another article.

Tapping the Back icon would jump back to the point where you left the first article.

Screen Light: By sliding your finger along the scale you can adjust the brightness on the screen. To use a higher light setting tap the + button and use the – button to use a lower light setting. To turn the light to minimum brightness press and hold the – button. Press and hold the + button for maximum light brightness. You can also touch anywhere on the light scale to select a specific setting.

Kindle Store: To shop the Kindle Store tap this button. Your Kindle must have an active 3G connection or active Wi-Fi to use this feature.

Search: To bring up the search field tap this button. Tap the X on the right side of the bar to exit search.

Menu button: To display a list of options tap this button. The menus are contextual, which means they change to offer appropriate options depending on what you're currently doing with the device. For example, on the Home screen of a Kindle with Special Offers, menu options may include Settings, Check for items, Create New Collection, Sync, Shop Kindle Store, View Special Offers, List or Cover View and Experimental Browser. Note that you can view content on the Home screen using the default cover view or by list view.

When you're reading a book, menu items specific to book reading include Book Description, Landscape or Portrait Mode, Vocabulary Builder, Reading Progress, and About the Author. (Note that the 'About the Author' feature is only available for books that include author profiles.)

About the Reading toolbar

When you are reading any book, tapping at the top of the screen reveals the Reading toolbar, as shown in the following illustration.

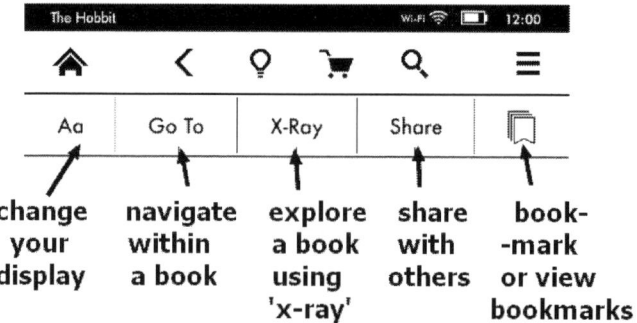

Text (Aa): Tap to display a dialog box containing text and font options for your books. You can change the font, font style, font size, line spacing or the margins used to display your text.

Go To: Tapping here displays a book's table of contents, including a 'Beginning' link (to move to the start of the book) and chapter titles. Use the Page or Location option to further navigate your book. The options displayed will vary depending on the content you're reading. Tap the Notes tab to access your notes and highlights. You can also view Popular highlights and Public notes by selecting the corresponding options under the Notes tab.

X-Ray: This feature lets you explore the "innards" of the book, akin to the way an x-ray gives you a peek "inside" a human body. As an example, you could examine every portion of a book that refers to a certain character or a location in a given city. (Note that the X-ray feature must be enabled by the book's publisher. If the feature is not enabled for a given book, the option appears dimmed within the toolbar.)

Share: Touch the Share icon to share your opinions about what you are reading with other readers via Twitter or Facebook.

Bookmarks: Touch to add or delete a bookmark on the current page, and to view previously added bookmarks. The Bookmark button on the toolbar changes from white to black while you are viewing bookmarked pages. A preview pane displays when you tap a bookmark in your list of existing bookmarks, and you can go to the bookmark location by tapping the bookmark within the preview pane. To exit the bookmark feature, tap anywhere outside the list of bookmarks.

About the Reading Navigation toolbar

While reading, you can swipe up from the bottom of the page to display the Reading Navigation toolbar, shown in the following illustration.

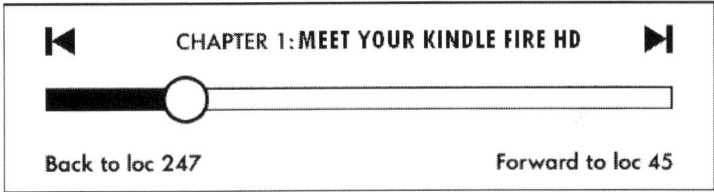

Use this toolbar to quickly move through a book by moving the slider left or right. As you move the slider, a preview of the corresponding location appears in a preview window. Tap the 'X' in the upper-right corner of the preview window to close the window and move to that location within the book.

About the Periodicals toolbar

When you're reading a periodical, the toolbars are configured specifically for that purpose. To display the toolbar, touch the top of the screen.

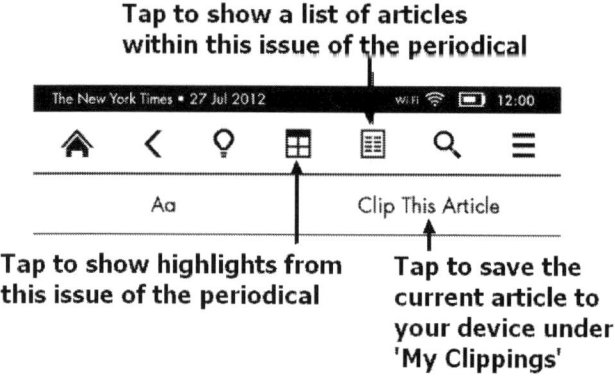

Periodical Home button: Touch to display highlights of the issue you're reading.

Articles and Sections button: Touch to go to the content list of sections and articles in a magazine or newspaper. (Note that this option is not available in blogs.)

A secondary toolbar is available when you're reading a periodical and are on the article detail page. Your options on the secondary toolbar include the following:

Text (Aa): Touch to display text and font options for your periodicals, including typeface, font size, margins and line spacing.

Clip This Article: Touch to clip an entire periodical article to the My Clippings File. The My Clippings file is located on your Home screen and stores your clipped articles, as well as any notes, bookmarks, and highlights.

About the Status indicators

At the top of the Home screen, in a narrow black band just above the Home screen toolbar, you'll see indicators that inform you about the status of your Kindle Paperwhite, as shown in the following illustration. To view these indicators within a book or document, touch the top of screen to display the toolbars, and the status indicators will appear directly above the toolbars.

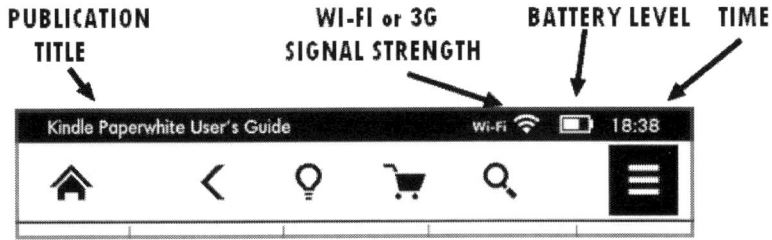

Wi-Fi / 3G Signal Strength indicator

The Wi-Fi / 3G signal strength indicator displays the relative strength of the signal from the Wi-Fi or cellular network currently used by your Paperwhite. The more bars on the Wi-Fi or 3G signal strength indicator that are filled, the stronger the signal. (On models equipped with the 3G option, you may see an icon for a GPRS or EDGE network next to the signal strength bars.

If you see a symbol in the shape of a jet aircraft in place of the wireless strength indicator, this indicates that your device is in Airplane Mode and you have no wireless connectivity.

Battery Level indicator

The Battery Level indicator shows the current charge level of the battery. (Note that a weak wireless signal can drain your battery much faster than would normally occur, because your Kindle's Wi-Fi circuitry stays overly active, hunting for a good Wi-Fi signal.)

Activity indicator

This indicator appears in the upper left corner of you Kindle screen when it is connecting to a network, scanning in search of a Wi-Fi network, synchronizing your device contents with the Amazon cloud, downloading new content, opening a large file, or loading a web page.

Parental Controls indicator

This indicator appears when Parental Controls are enabled for your Kindle Paperwhite. Parental Controls let you restrict access to the Kindle Store, Experimental Web Browser, and content stored under your account in the Amazon cloud. Parents can use this feature to prevent children from viewing inappropriate online content, or from purchasing content without the parents' permission.

Changing your Paperwhite Settings

Before moving on to successive chapters that will give you more details on the many ways that you can use your Paperwhite, you'll likely find it helpful to know how to access the most commonly-used settings. Go to your Home screen, tap the Menu icon, and choose Settings from the menu that appears, as shown in this illustration.

Once you choose Settings, the following screen appears:

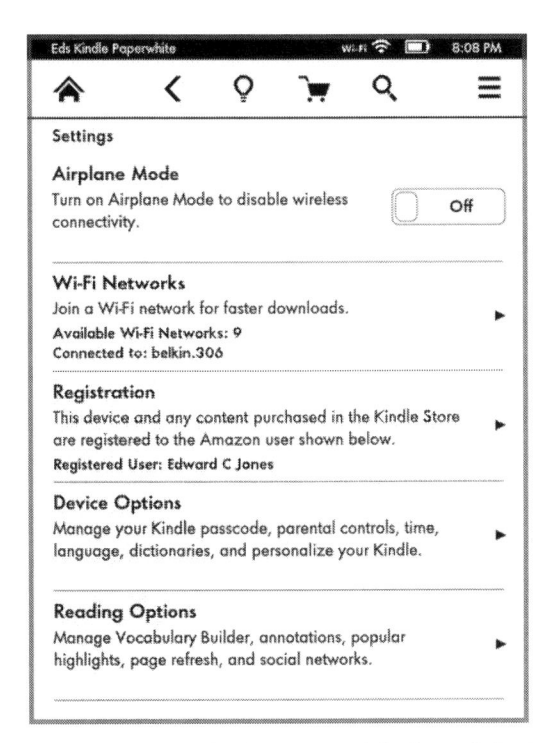

Airplane Mode: Turn on Airplane Mode to disable Wi-Fi connectivity when in flight, or whenever you are out of range of a Wi-Fi signal.

Wi-Fi Networks: Tap this option to display a list of available Wi-Fi networks. Once the list appears, you can tap any entry within the list, and enter a password if the network is secured, in order to connect.

Registration: You can use this option to visually check your Kindle Paperwhite registration information, or to de-register your device if you plan to give or sell it to another.

Device options: Tap this choice to reveal a screen that lets you set a number of device specific options; these are detailed throughout this chapter. These include options to set password protection on your device, to set up parental controls, to reset the date and time, to choose your language, and to personalize your device.

Reading options: Tap this choice to display a number of reading options for your Kindle Paperwhite. These include a vocabulary builder that remembers dictionary look ups, a page refresh option, a social network options that lets you add your Twitter or Facebook accounts, and a Notes and Highlights option that lets you manage annotations, public notes, and popular highlights.

Chapter 3: Let's Go Shopping!

Amazon has integrated the Kindle Paperwhite line to provide a first class shopping experience through the Amazon stores. (The phrase 'stores', plural, is intentional, because with the company's growth, Amazon has divided their online retail store into a collection of stores.) You can think of it as having all o0f the convenience of a mall-- different stores, each specializing in carrying a broad assortment of products in a specific area-- with none of the disadvantages of a mall (noisy crowds, unruly teenagers, or bad food at the food court). At the time of this writing, Amazon has divided its digital stores into eight categories: books, music, videos, newsstand, apps, games, audiobooks, and Amazon Prime. At the Home screen, tap Shop, and you will see links for the different stores on the page that appears, as shown in the following illustration.

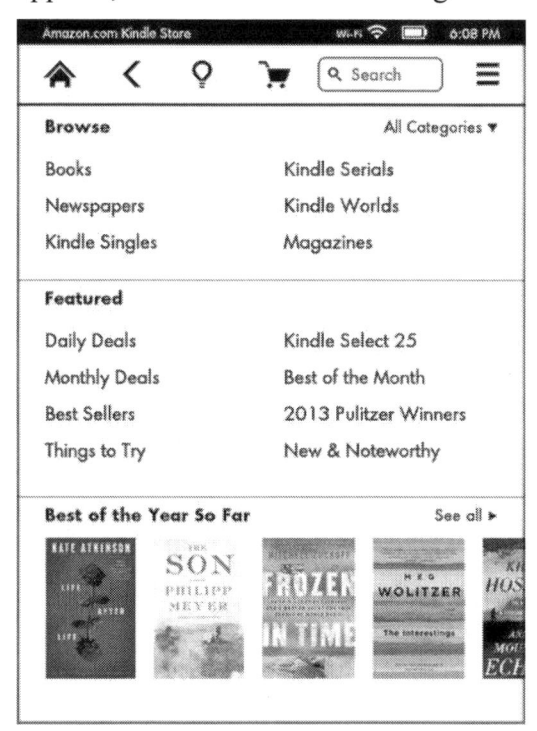

To make shopping easier, you will probably want to set up 1- click ordering as a payment method. 1 Click ordering places your order automatically, letting you skip the hassle of a digital shopping cart. When you place your first order at Amazon and enter a payment method and shipping address, 1-Click ordering is enabled automatically. If you click Buy now with 1-Click on any product page, your order is automatically charged to the default payment method registered to your account, and it is shipped to the default address.

You can also use 1-click to ship to multiple shipping addresses. Perhaps you wish to have some items shipped to you at your job, others at your primary home, and some at your vacation home. Login to your Amazon account through a web browser, and click Manage Your Account. At the next screen, click Manage Addresses and 1-Click Settings. At the next screen that appears, you can enter more than one shipping address.

When you save multiple shipping addresses, and you order an item, a list box with all of your addresses will appear. You can then choose the desired address to have the item shipped to that location.

Note: You must have cookies enabled within your computers' web browser to use 1-Click shopping. ("Cookies" are small chunks of data stored by your browser which are used by Amazon, as well as by many online banks and stores, to identify your account). If you have not enabled cookies within your browser, you can still purchase items by adding them to the Amazon Shopping Cart, and clicking Proceed to checkout when you are ready to complete your order.

Buying Items

Once you've connected wirelessly and you've set up your 1-click payment option at Amazon, you can easily purchase books, magazines, and newspapers from Amazon, and automatically download your purchases to your Kindle Paperwhite. Tap at the top of the screen and tap the Home 🏠 icon to get to your Home screen, then tap Shop (the icon in the shape of a shopping cart), and the Amazon Kindle Store will appear on your screen, as shown in the illustration earlier in this chapter. You can browse among the various categories or search for items using the Search box at the upper right. Once you've located a desired item, you can tap Buy to download the book or periodical, or you can tap Try a Sample to download the start of the book for free.

Once you purchase an item, it is stored in your own library in the Amazon Cloud, and you can download it to any other Kindles that you may own. You can also read your purchases using any of the free Kindle Readings Apps available for most personal computers and smartphones.

About Amazon Prime

If you do a lot of shopping at Amazon, and assuming you are a resident of the U.S., it is probably worth your while to sign up for Amazon Prime. Amazon Prime is a subscription-based member service. At the time of this writing, the service costs $99.00 per year. In return for the yearly membership fee, Amazon Prime members receive a number of benefits, not the least of which is free two-day standard shipping on eligible items, free access to Amazon Instant Video, and the ability to borrow books from the Kindle Owners Lending Library. (I can highly recommend the service, and no, I'm not being paid by Amazon to say this. If one orders a fair amount from Amazon, the savings on shipping costs alone will more than justify the annual membership fee.)

Where's My Data? (Your Kindle Paperwhite Storage, and the Amazon Cloud)

With the popularity of tablets, you may have heard talk of what may be a somewhat magical and mystical place known as "the cloud." Your Kindle Paperwhite has some built-in data storage, ranging from 8 gigabytes to 32 gigabytes, depending upon the model of Kindle Paperwhite that you purchased.

This may sound like a lot of space, but in the grand scheme of things, it really is not. (By comparison, the average personal computer sold at the time of this writing typically has a 250 gigabyte or 500 gigabyte hard drive, and a single Blu-Ray DVD movie occupies roughly 25 gigabytes.) If you tried to store massive amounts of digital content, such as well over the estimated maximum of around 1100 e-books, you would exhaust the Paperwhite's usable space. To get around this problem, the Kindle Paperwhite (and many other e-readers) store large amounts of information in the cloud, which is another name for data servers that are accessed from the Internet. Amazon's servers are referred to as the Amazon Cloud, and all Kindle Paperwhite owners have access to unlimited amounts of data storage for their purchases in the Amazon cloud.

Content that you purchase from Amazon is stored in either of two places: in your cloud storage on Amazon's servers, and on your Kindle Paperwhite itself. (Often, your content is stored in two places simultaneously: when you download an item, it is stored both on your device and a copy of it remains in the Amazon cloud.) When you initially purchase a book (even free content is purchased, you just aren't charged for this), the content is initially stored in your personal space in the Amazon Cloud, where the content is not taking up any space on your Kindle Paperwhite. When you press the Download button that appears on the icon for that content in the cloud, it gets downloaded to the memory space of your Kindle Paperwhite itself.)

If you tap the top of the screen on your Kindle Paperwhite and then tap the Home 🏠 icon to get to the Home screen, at the top left (just underneath the Home icon) you will see icons for Cloud and On Device, as shown in the illustration that follows.

Tap Cloud to see all of the content that is stored on Amazon's cloud under your account, and tap On Device to see all the content that you downloaded from the cloud onto your device. You can download content from the cloud onto your device anytime you have an active Wi-Fi connection, and you can delete content from the device as necessary to ensure that you have plenty of room for new content.

Removing books from your device

Remove books you've finished reading to save on storage space. If you are done with a particular book, you can remove the book from your Kindle Paperwhite.

(The book remains in your personal space within the Amazon cloud, so you can always download the same book at a later time if you would like to re-read the text.

To remove the book from your Paperwhite, press Home, locate the book on your Home screen, and perform a 'long press' on the icon for the book. From the popup menu that appears, choose 'Remove from Device.'

Have Paperwhite, Will Travel

The Paperwhite makes for an ideal travel companion, if for no other reason than that a single battery charge will outlast the longest of plane flights and make for less stress when waiting in those boarding lines at the Hartsfield or at Heathrow. Some travel trips for the Paperwhite include the following:

For the security scan at the terminal, the security agents will probably want to see the device powered up. Turn on the Paperwhite and place it in the plastic bin alongside your wallet/purse and keys.

Before boarding, turn on Airplane Mode. Touch at the top of the screen, touch the Menu ☰ icon at the upper right, touch Settings, and turn on Airplane Mode. And be sure to completely power down the device during take offs and landings.

Also keep in mind that "airplane mode" isn't just useful on aircraft. If you are on a cruise or on a long distance road or rail trip, you may want to turn on Airplane Mode if you know you aren't in range of a Wi-Fi signal. Doing so will noticeably increase your battery life, because the Paperwhite's Wi-Fi circuitry won't stay overly active hunting for a non-existent Wi-Fi network.

If you travel outside of your home country, make sure you have any electrical adapters needed for the power outlets in the country where you are headed, and if you do a lot of travel by car, consider getting a USB Car Charger that plugs into your vehicle's cigarette lighter. These are relatively inexpensive, and can be obtained from Amazon or from major retailers such as Radio Shack, Best Buy, and Wal-Mart.

The Best Things in Life are (Often!) Free

Of course, any power user of the Kindle Paperwhite should be well aware of the fact that spending money is not the only way to obtain books and other content for your device. The next chapter will look at a number of ways that you can obtain thousands of books and digital documents, at a cost of no more than your time and effort.

Chapter 4: Free Books for your Kindle Paperwhite

Your Kindle Paperwhite is a great source of reading, but let's face it: content costs, and quality contents costs more. Like everyone else, authors and editors certainly expect to eat (no surprise there), and marketing costs skyrocket when you get into the league of big-name authors and the costs of advertising those New York Times bestsellers that you're fond of reading. But there are great sources of free, quality content available for your Kindle Paperwhite. My favorite source is one that in a way, you've likely already paid for (and continue paying for) over the years: I'm speaking of your tax-supported, local public library.

How to Get Free Books from your Public Library

One great source of free content for your Kindle Paperwhite may require a visit to your local public library (and if you possess a valid library card, that single trip may not be necessary). Many Kindle owners are oblivious to the fact that most public libraries now loan books (as well as movies, music, and other digital content) for the Amazon Kindle line of e-readers and tablets, as well as for other digital products like smartphones, Apple iPads, and other tablet computers.

First, go to the website of your local library. (If you don't know the website for your local library, you should be able to find this with a simple Google search.) Once you are at the website for your local library, look for a sidebar link that says "borrow e-books/digital downloads" or something similar. Click this page, and you will typically be taken to another page that explains how you can borrow and download e-books and other digital content from your local library. (The following illustration shows the page that exists for my local library in Charlotte, North Carolina.)

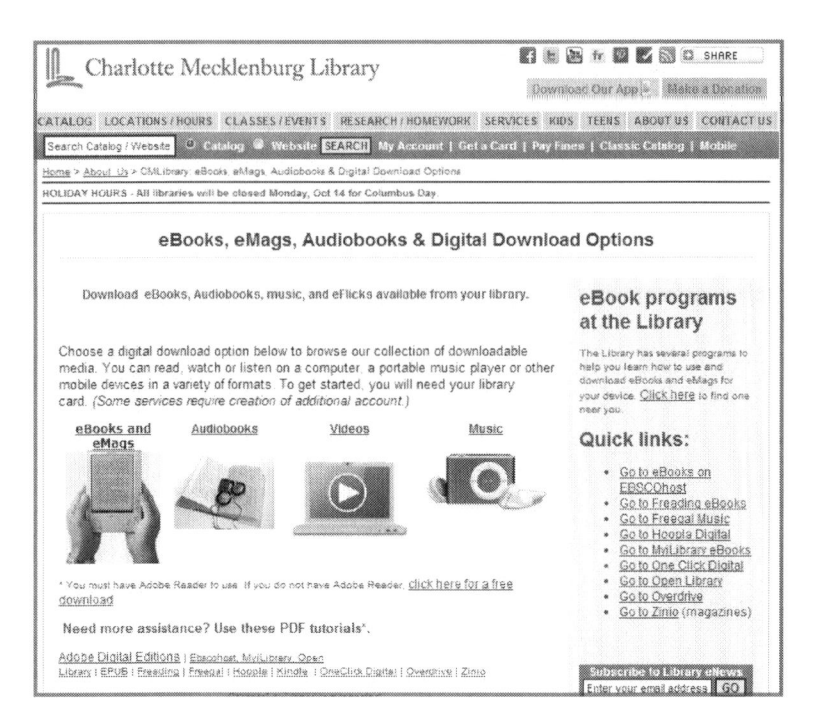

Most libraries will require you to log in using your library card number, and you may have to download e-books to your computer as Adobe PDF files. Once you download the file, you can e-mail the book to your Kindle using the "Send to Kindle" feature described in the following chapter. You can also use the file transfer techniques described in the next chapter to place the file in your Documents folder of your Kindle Paperwhite.

If your city does not support the loaning of e-books, there are libraries that allow nonresidents to obtain a library card for an annual fee. Two, at the time of this writing, are those of Fairfax County, Virginia (www.fairfaxcounty.gov/library for more information) and the City of Philadelphia (www.freelibrary.org for more information).

Different libraries have different lending policies, so you'll want to check with your local library to determine the exact length of your loan. (Most libraries that support downloads of Adobe files use the 'Adobe Secure PDF' format, enabling the e-book to "turn into a pumpkin", so to speak, at the end of the loan period.) In my resident town of Charlotte, North Carolina, books have a two-week loan with one possible renewal. Many libraries now offer regularly scheduled classes or workshops that teach library patrons how to download digital content, so you may want to visit your local library and sign up for such a class in your home town.

Amazon Prime and the Kindle Owner's Lending Library

Another great source of free books is the Kindle Owners' Lending Library, a service that Amazon makes available to Kindle owners who have also enrolled in Amazon Prime. If you are a member of Amazon Prime, you owe it to yourself to check out the Kindle Owners' Lending Library. The Kindle Owners Lending Library allows Amazon Prime members to borrow one book at a time each month, at no cost. There are thousands of books available through the service, and you can find free books to borrow through the Kindle Owners Lending Library using these steps:

1. At the Kindle Paperwhite store, click "See all categories." When the list of various categories (Books, Kindle Singles, Kindle Newsstand, New & Noteworthy, etc.) appears, click the Kindle Owners' Lending Library option.

2. After picking the Kindle Owners' Lending Library, you can browse a list of books to borrow. You will know that a book is eligible for borrowing because it will have a "Prime" badge attached.

3. Click the 'Borrow' tab. Next, you'll see a "Buy for $xx.xx" tab and a "Borrow for Free" tab. Click the "Borrow for Free" tab, and your borrowed book will be downloaded to your Kindle Paperwhite.

Finding dozens of great free books with the "search on zero" trick

A third great way to find free books is to search for... free books! As part of regular ongoing promotions, many authors will place their books on sale for nothing during certain days of a 90-day period, as part of an authors' program called Amazon KDP Select. You can take advantage of this fact by simply searching among any desired genre of Kindle books, and entering "0.00" as your search criteria in the Search box. What appears will be every Kindle book that has a price of zero dollars, zero cents on that particular day. This list of books will change wildly on a daily basis, so if you're an avid reader, you may find it worth your while to perform this sort of a search on a regular basis.

Download Free Books from the Web for your Kindle Paperwhite

The final source of free books that this chapter will detail is that of the Internet itself. You can find countless sources of free e-books on the Internet. These come in a variety of file formats; besides its own native file format of Kindle (.azw) files, your Kindle Paperwhite will also read books in Adobe Acrobat (.PDF) format, in MobiPocket (.MOBI) format, or in plain text (.TXT) format. Unfortunately, your Kindle Paperwhite will NOT read files in the popular E-PUB format used by the Sony e-reader, the Barnes and Noble NOOK, and many other e-readers. The solution for this is not overwhelmingly complex; you can download free e-book converter programs that will convert e-books from most other formats into Amazon's Kindle (.KZW) format. An excellent program is called Calibre (go to www.calibre-ebook.com for details). Calibre can convert files from many formats, including the E-PUB format, into the Amazon Kindle file format. Once you convert the file, use the file transfer techniques described in the next chapter of this book, to transfer the e-books that you've converted to your Kindle Paperwhite.

As for sources, performing a Google search for "free e-books" will return an avalanche of sites. Here is a small list to get you started:

Project Gutenberg- www.gutenberg.org

ManyBooks.net- http://manybooks.net

Google Books- http://books.google.com/

MobiPocket Free Books- www.mobipocket.com/freebooks/

An exhaustive source of free computer-based books can be found at http://freecomputerbooks.com. Finally, you'll find a surprisingly comprehensive list of textbooks that can be legally shared, at http://textbookrevolution.org. These are in .PDF format.

Once you've downloaded free boos from the web, you'll need a way to get those books onto your Kindle Paperwhite. Read on, as that is the subject of the following chapter.

Chapter 5: Open your Kindle Paperwhite to the World by Managing Files

In press reviews, Amazon Kindles have taken a fair share of criticism for being a relatively "closed ecosystem," according to critics. Many reviewers have claimed that Kindle owners are dependent on purchasing virtually all content from Amazon. In the opinion of this author, that reputation is somewhat undeserved. Certainly, it is in Amazon's interest to get you to buy your content from Amazon. But the 'closed ecosystem' claim made by many members of the press implies that you must purchase all your content from Amazon, and that is simply not the case. In addition to purchasing content from the Amazon store, you can find millions (literally!) of books from other sources, and these can be copied to your Kindle Paperwhite from your computer using the USB cable that is a part of your charging assembly. The Kindle Paperwhite can load files stored under the .mobi file format for its e-books, and e-books in the .mobi format can be found in thousands of places all over the internet, some paid, and others free. There are also millions of books in the popular E-PUB format used by Sony and by Google, and there are free converters readily available from hundreds of sources on the web that will convert files from the E-PUB format into the .mobi format usable by all Amazon Kindles.

You can also email documents directly to your Kindle Paperwhite, using Amazon's free Send to Kindle service. Every registered Kindle has its own assigned email address, and you can send Microsoft Word documents, rich text (RTF) or text (TXT) files, and Adobe PDF files to your Kindle Paperwhite's assigned email address. Within roughly 5 minutes of the time that you send a file as an attachment, it will show up on your Kindle Paperwhite, in the Documents folder. You can then tap the document to open it and read it on your Kindle.

To take full advantage of all of these features of the Kindle Paperwhite, you'll need to know how to use the file management features of the Kindle Paperwhite. You'll find various techniques that pertain to these topics covered throughout this chapter.

Send Files to Your Kindle Paperwhite via E-Mail

If you purchased your Kindle Paperwhite directly from Amazon, it was registered for you when it arrived. If you purchased it from a retailer such as Best Buy, you may have gone through the setup steps on your own. In either case, your Kindle Paperwhite has been assigned a Send to Kindle email address. This address is something similar to username@kindle.com. To see your email address, get to your Home screen, and tap the Menu ☰ icon at the upper-right, and tap Settings. When the Settings screen appears, tap Device Options, then tap Personalize My Kindle. You will see a screen similar to the following example:

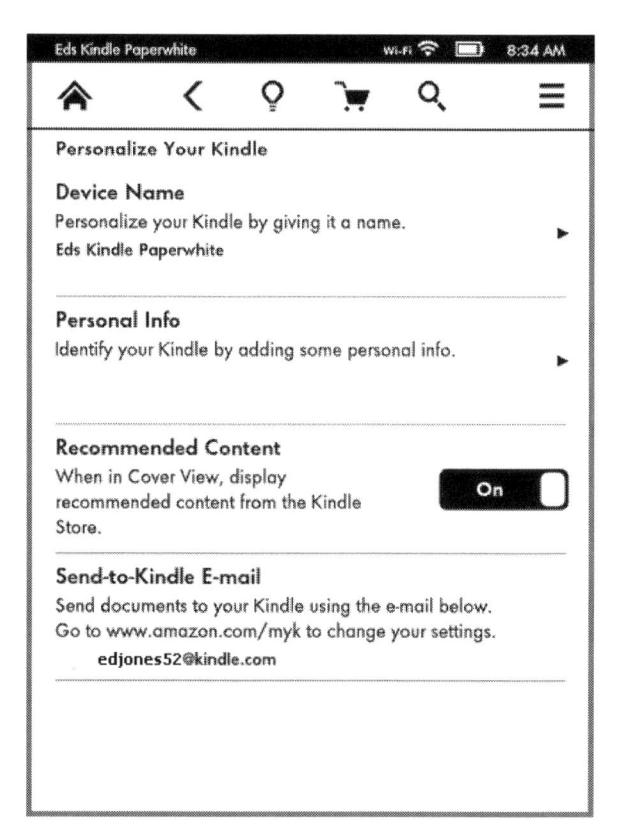

At the bottom of this screen, your Kindle's e-mail address will be listed under "Send to Kindle E-mail." The address will take on a format similar to username@kindle.com, where 'username' is a name that was assigned to your Kindle at the time of its registration. This is the email address that you can use to send files as attachments to your Kindle Paperwhite.

Before you can send any documents to your Kindle Paperwhite, you must add the sending email address to an "Approved personal document email list" under your Amazon account settings. To prevent Kindle owners from receiving unwanted spam, Amazon blocks any email sent to a Kindle address at Kindle.com that hasn't been added to the approved personal document email list. Log into your Amazon account in a computer's web browser, and under

55

the 'Your Account' link, click 'Manage Your Kindle.' At the next screen that appears, you'll see all your Kindle devices (assuming you own more than one). If you own just your Kindle Paperwhite, you will see just that device. Scroll down and locate the desired Kindle in your list of devices, click the Edit link to the right of the device name, and you will be able to change the e-mail address registered to that Kindle. You can also add authorized e-mail addresses that will be permitted to send e-mail to your Kindle. By default, Amazon adds the e-mail address that is associated with your Amazon account. To add authorized addresses, under 'Your Kindle Account' at the left, click Personal Document Settings, and then look for the Approved Personal Document E-mail List near the bottom of the screen. You can click the 'Add a new Approved E-mail Address' link in this area to add another email address.

Attaching Word Documents, PDF Files, and Pictures to E-Mails Sent to Your Kindle Paperwhite

Once you've added your email address to the approved personal document email list, you can attach files to an email message and send it to your send to kindle address. Documents can be in the form of .DOC, .DOCX, .RTF, .TXT, .HTM or .HTML, PDF, .MOBI' and .AZW file formats. Images can be sent in the .JPG, .PNG, .GIF, or .BMP file formats. The conversion process assumes an active Wi-Fi connection, since Amazon's Send to Kindle service converts your file into Amazon's own .AZW file format, then downloads it to your Kindle Paperwhite using Amazon's Whispernet.

NOTE: Attachments cannot be larger than 50 megabytes per attachment, and each email must not have more than 25 attachments. If any of your files are larger than 50 megabytes, the Send to Kindle process will fail for that file, and that file will not appear in your Documents folder.

Copying Files from a Computer to Your Kindle Paperwhite

You can also copy files from a laptop or desktop computer to your Kindle Paperwhite, using a USB to micro-USB cable. This is the same cable that is supplied as a charging cable for your Kindle Paperwhite; one end contains the micro USB connector that plugs into the base of your Kindle Paperwhite, and the other end contains a standard USB connector. Use the cable to connect your Kindle Paperwhite to your computer, and the Paperwhite will appear as a USB flash drive under your computer's operating system.

Create a new folder on your computer's hard drive, and name the folder the same name that you would like to see appear for the book or document name on the Home screen of your Paperwhite. Copy the e-book, Word document, Adobe PDF, or other acceptable file type into the new folder, then use the techniques described in the paragraphs that follow to move or copy the new folder into the /Documents folder of your Kindle Paperwhite.

Users of Windows XP may have to install additional software before using a USB cable to access the Kindle Paperwhite, and the users of the Apple Mac will have to install additional software. Go to the following link for additional details:

http://www.kindle.com/support/downloads

Once the Kindle Paperwhite appears as a USB drive under your computer's operating system, you can simply drag and drop or copy and paste the desired files into the appropriate folders of the Kindle Paperwhite.

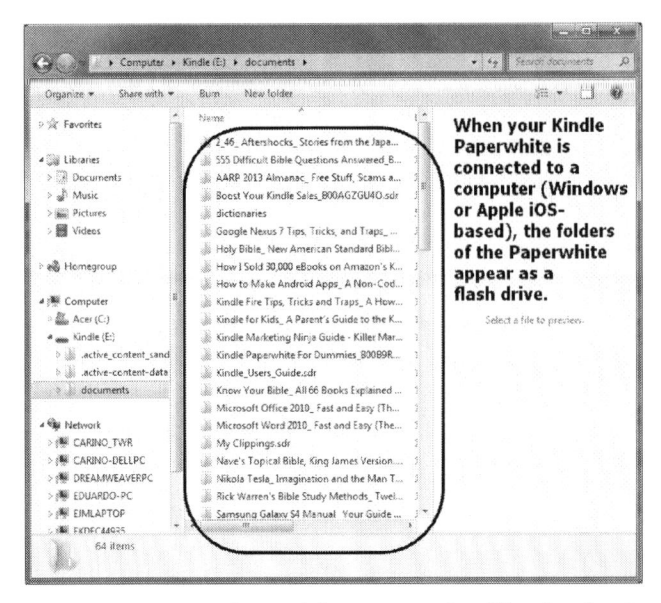

When your Kindle Paperwhite is connected to a computer (Windows or Apple iOS-based), the folders of the Paperwhite appear as a flash drive.

You can use a USB cable to transfer files in the form of .DOC, .DOCX, .XLS, .PPT, .RTF, .TXT, .HTM or .HTML, PDF, .MOBI' and .AZW file formats. Images can be in the .JPG, .PNG, .GIF, or .BMP file formats.

Once you connect the Kindle Paperwhite to your computer, you can navigate to the folder that appears under the device name /Kindle within your File Explorer. Within the /Kindle device, locate and open the /Documents folder. (An example of the author's /Documents folder is shown in the center area of the above illustration.) Open another window containing the new folder with the file that you want to place on your Kindle Paperwhite, and use standard drag-and-drop or Edit/Copy and Edit/Paste techniques to move or copy the folder from your computer to your Kindle Paperwhite.

After compatible files have been transferred using the USB cable or sent to your Paperwhite using the 'Send to Kindle' e-mail address, those files will appear on your Home screen, similar to the examples shown in the following illustration.

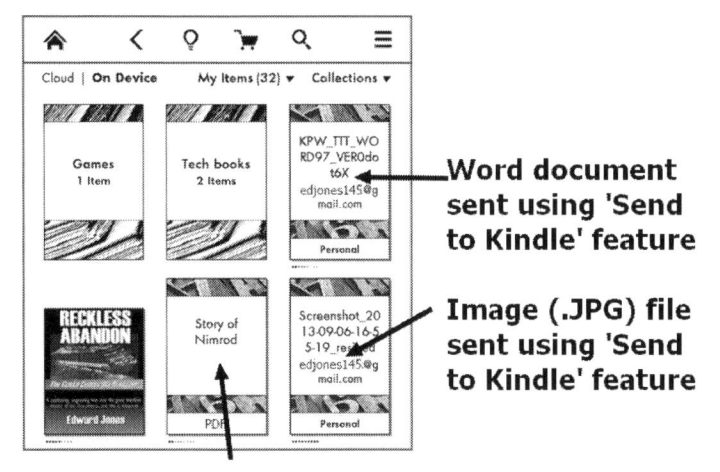

Word document sent using 'Send to Kindle' feature

Image (.JPG) file sent using 'Send to Kindle' feature

Adobe .PDF file transferred from computer to Paperwhite using USB cable

If you copied the file to the /Documents folder of your Paperwhite, the file appears named after the folder you copied into the /Documents folder (or it takes on the actual filename, if you simply copied a file into the root of the /Documents folder). If you used Amazon's Send to Kindle feature to send the file as an attachment, it appears with a name based on the filename, and the type of file indicated at the bottom of the dialog box. In either case, you can tap the icon representing the item to open the file or document.

Chapter 6: Getting online with the web browser

The Paperwhite may have been designed from the ground up as an e-reader, but it does also have the capability to surf the web (and lets you stay in contact via e-mail, using the web browser to access your web-based e-mail accounts). Before proceeding, a few words of warning are appropriate. The web browser in the Kindle Paperwhite is called an "Experimental Browser," and it's called by that moniker for a reason. The browser is slow, and prone to far more crashes than the average web browser. The Paperwhite browser also has the following known limitations:

- The browser will not play videos
- The browser does not support Shockwave or Flash embedded content
- The browser does not support Java animations

Once you accept the limitations, the browser is a better option than no option at all, so this chapter details the use of the experimental browser, and offers tips on how you can use the web browser to check your web-based e-mail.

To use the Paperwhite browser, first get to your Home screen (tap the top of the screen, and tap the Home icon). Next, tap the Menu icon to display the Home screen options menu. When the menu opens, tap Experimental Browser. In a moment, a browser window appears, similar to the example shown in the following illustration.

By default, the Experimental Browser displays the web page that you last visited when using the browser. (If you've never used the browser, a mobile-friendly version of the Amazon home page appears.) You can tap within the web address/URL field, and enter a desired website using the keyboard that appears.

Creating and Using Bookmarks

Bookmark commonly visited pages so you can return to them quickly at a later time. As with all modern web browsers, the Experimental Browser provides the ability to bookmark sites so that you can easily return to the same site. To add a bookmark, get to the desired web page, tap the Menu icon at the upper right, and choose 'Bookmark this Page' from the menu that appears.

To get to any of your saved bookmarks, with the web browser open, tap the Menu icon at the upper right, and tap 'Bookmarks.' A list of bookmarks appears, and you can tap the desired bookmark to go directly to that page.

To edit a bookmark, with the web browser open, tap the Menu icon at the upper right, and choose 'Bookmarks.' When the list of bookmarks appears, tap 'Edit' at the lower right, then tap the desired bookmark in the list to edit the name for the bookmark.

To delete a bookmark, with the web browser open, tap the Menu icon at the upper right, and tap 'Bookmarks.' When the list of bookmarks appears, tap 'Remove' at the bottom of the list, and you will see check marks appear beside each bookmark. Turn on the check boxes for every bookmark you wish to delete, and then tap 'Remove' at the bottom of the list to delete the selected bookmarks.

Changing the Browser Settings

There are a limited number of settings that you can change to suit your tastes (not surprising, given that the browser itself is fairly limited). With any web page open, tap the Menu icon at the upper right, and choose 'Browser Settings' from the menu that appears. The dialog box that opens provides four settings: Clear History, Clear Cookies, Disable JavaScript, and Disable Images.

Clear History: The experimental browser saves a history of websites that you've visited, in order to speed up the load time when you revisit those same pages. You can use the Clear History option to delete this information.

Clear Cookies: Cookies are routinely used by many websites to store personal information such as your email address or a login password. You can use the Clear Cookies option to delete this stored information from your browser.

Disable JavaScript: Many web sites use JavaScript as part of a website's design. And while the experimental browser does not support Java applets, it does support JavaScript. You can turn on the Disable JavaScript option to disable the use of JavaScript, which may result in a faster display for certain websites.

Disable Images: Use this option to disable the loading of graphics and images, which can speed up your website displays by showing only the text of the website.

Sending and receiving E-Mail with the browser

If you use web-based e-mail through a service like Google's gMail, Microsoft's Live (formerly Hotmail), or Yahoo Mail, you can use the Paperwhite browser to read and reply to your e-mail. With the stripped-down and feature-limited browser that's built into the Paperwhite, the secret to success is to use the mobile-friendly versions of the providers' web-based mail sites. The addresses that you'll want to enter into the address field of the browser are as follows:

For Google's gMail	m.gmail.com
For Windows Live	m.live.com
For Yahoo Mail	m.yahoo.com

Enter the address shown, and a mobile-device friendly version of the provider's site will appear. (The following illustration shows the mobile version of Google's gMail site when displayed in the Paperwhite's web browser.)

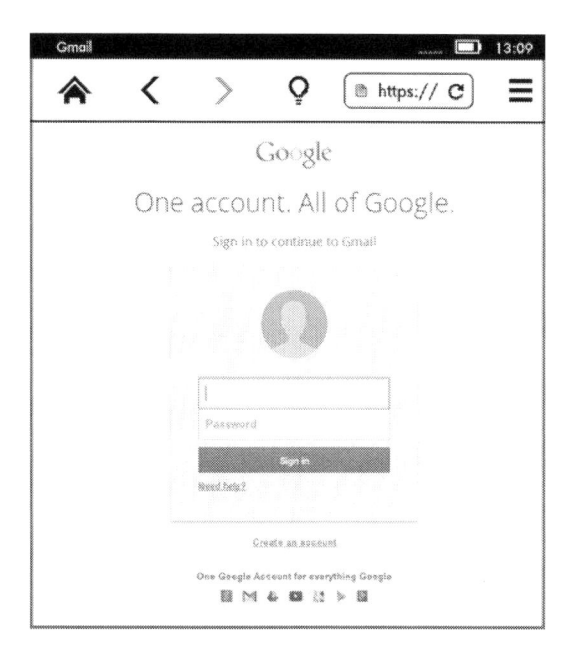

Given the limitations of the browser, you will not be able to work with attachments. Still, if you just need to read or reply to a simple e-mail, the Paperwhite's experimental browser will provide sufficient power to get the job done.

Chapter 7: Security Tips, Tricks, and Traps

With the Kindle Paperwhite, Amazon has combined an extremely well-designed e-reader with the near-flawless customer service experience that makes for shopping with the company, and the result makes for a consumer experience that, as far as ease of use is concerned, is hard to beat. That same design advantage, in the wrong hands, could be a major security risk. For that reason, this chapter provides some tips on securing your Kindle Paperwhite.

Lock your Kindle Paperwhite. An unlocked Kindle Paperwhite is somewhat akin to an unlocked car with the keys left in the ignition. If you lose your Kindle Paperwhite, or the device is stolen, whoever happens to "acquire" it could leave comments on your Facebook or Twitter accounts, and possibly order and download a number of e-books from Amazon before you became aware of the loss. You can set a login password to prevent unauthorized users from gaining access to the machine's content. At the Home screen, tap the Menu icon at the upper-right then tap Settings in the menu that appears. At the next screen, tap Device Options, then tap Device Passcode. Enter a password, then enter it a second time to confirm.

Make a note of your password in a secure location, if you are the type that forgets passwords. If you do lock down your Kindle Paperwhite and you forget the password, the only way to restore operation of the device is to perform a default factory reset, which will also erase all of your existing settings and take the machine back to the factory "out of the box" condition.

Back up your machine's settings to the Amazon Cloud on a regular basis. You can easily backup your device settings simply by using the Sync feature found in the Menu options of the Home screen. Every so often (perhaps monthly), at the Home screen, tap the Menu icon, and tap 'Sync and Check for Items' in the menu that appears. Doing so will not only synchronize things such as your purchased content, but also the general settings for the device will be backed up to your account in the Amazon Cloud. This way, if the device ever needs replacing, you will save a significant amount of time as you will be able to pull your settings from the Amazon Cloud down into the replacement device.

Restrict purchasing and browsing with Parental Controls. If you have young ones around the house that also use your Kindle Paperwhite, you may want to turn on parental controls to prevent young ones from surfing the web's more inappropriate locations, and to prevent their making unauthorized purchases as well. At the Home screen, tap the Menu icon at the upper-right then tap Settings in the menu that appears. At the next screen, tap Device Options, then tap Parental Controls. You will see a Parental Controls screen with options for disabling access to the web browser, access to the Kindle Store, and access to the Amazon cloud. Tap the corresponding On / Off button beside each option to enable (or disable) access.

Note that when Parental Controls are enabled, the De-Registration and Reset Device options are disabled. Also, if you disable access to the Kindle Store, you can continue to buy books by using a web browser on your computer to log into your Amazon account.

Chapter 8: Battery and Power Tips, Tricks, and Traps

One of the many strong points of the Kindle Paperwhite is its battery life. The e-ink display of a Kindle Paperwhite allows the device to run for weeks at an average of 3 hours daily use between recharges. But there are specific tips that can help you get more out of your Kindle Paperwhite's battery life and go for longer periods of time between charges.

tip! Dim the screen, lengthen the battery life. Much of the power consumed by your Kindle Paperwhite goes toward powering the built-in backlighting, and the brighter the screen is lit, the more power that gets consumed. So when you're seated in that cramped tin can called an airliner at 30,000 feet, on that brutal nonstop from London to Los Angeles, turn down the brightness. At the Home screen, tap the Screen Lighting icon near the center of the toolbar (the one in the shape of a light bulb). Tap and drag the slider that appears down to a level that's comfortable for reading, then tap anywhere outside the dialog box to close it. Your battery will last longer, and you can always turn the brightness back up after you're at the hotel in Los Angeles.

tip! Shut down Wi-Fi when there's no chance of getting a Wi-Fi signal. In places where there is no chance of getting a working Wi-Fi signal (such as most commuter rail lines and most aircraft), the wireless circuitry inside your Kindle Paperwhite doesn't know any better and stays unusually active, checking for a Wi-Fi signal and consuming an abnormally high amount of battery power. An easy way to prevent this is to switch to Airplane mode, which disables the Paperwhite's Wi-Fi. (You will still be able to access any reading content you've already downloaded to your device.) At the Home screen, tap the Menu icon at the upper-right then tap Settings in the menu that appears. At the next screen, tap the Off/On indicator to the right of Airplane Mode. (When you are back in range of a strong Wi-Fi signal, remember to turn off Airplane Mode).

tip! Every so often, run down the battery on purpose. If you're the type of individual that keeps your rechargeable devices connected to a wall outlet, you may actually be shortening your battery life in the long run. The type of battery used by the Kindle Paperwhite (as is used by other tablets and most laptop computers) actually loses its effectiveness over time if it is constantly kept in a state of near-full charge. The way to prevent this is to perform what is called a "deep discharge"—you intentionally allow your battery to run down closer to the point of exhaustion before recharging your device. Doing this on a monthly basis will help keep your Kindle Paperwhite's battery working near top-notch condition.

CONCLUSION (and a favor to ask!)

I truly hope that you enjoy using your Kindle Paperwhite as much as I have enjoyed using mine and writing about the Paperwhite. As an author, I'd love to ask a favor: if you have the time, please consider writing a short review of this book. Honest reviews help me to write better books. You can post a review by going to Amazon.com, searching on the term 'Paperwhite Tips, Tricks and Traps by Edward Jones,' scrolling down the page and clicking the button that reads, "Write a Customer Review." And my sincere thanks for your time!

I do feel that Amazon's Kindle Paperwhite is the best e-reader that money can buy. Hopefully, after you have had the opportunity to try some of the many techniques that have been outlined in this guide, you'll discover that for yourself.

-Ed Jones

Join our mailing list...

We would be honored to add your name to our mailing list, where we can keep you informed of any book updates and of additional tips or topics about the Kindle Paperwhite. Our mailing list will NEVER be sold to others (because we hate spam as much as you probably do), and the only information that we will ask you to supply is a valid e-mail address.

Other books by the author: To visit the author's Amazon page for a complete list of books, visit the following website (note the underscore before the final word):

http://www.amazon.com/author/edwardjones_writer

Alternately, visit the author's website at www.thekindlewizard.com.

Kindle for Kids
A Parents' Guide to the Kindle Fire HD
FREE DIGITAL CONTENT
Google NEXUS 7
TIPS, TRICKS, and TRAPS
TOP 300 FREE APPS
KINDLE
Samsung GALAXY S4
TIPS, TRICKS, and TRAPS
Edward Jones
KINDLE FIRE HD
USER'S GUIDE
MICROSOFT OFFICE 2010
FAST & EASY
MICROSOFT PowerPoint
KINDLE FIRE HD
TIPS, TRICKS, and TRAPS
FREE BOOKS
MICROSOFT WORD
FAST&EASY
MICROSOFT EXCEL
FAST&EASY
MICROSOFT ACCESS 2010 ESSENTIALS
Get it Done
WordPress
FINISH
CREATING APPLICATIONS WITH MICROSOFT ACCESS 2010
Get it Done
MICROSOFT ACCESS
FAST&EASY
WORDPRESS FOR CHURCHES

Kindle Paperwhite Tips, Tricks, and Traps: A How-To Tutorial for the Kindle Paperwhite

by Edward Jones

© 16 June 2014 by Jones-Mack Technology Services of Charlotte, NC.

No part of this book may be reproduced, stored within a retrieval system, or transmitted without the express permission of the publisher. All rights reserved.

Printed in Great Britain
by Amazon